LIVING IN THE
WEALTHY
PLACE

A Road Map to Authentic Riches

MICHAEL & RAMONA WOODS

LIVING IN THE WEALTHY PLACE

A Road Map to Authentic Riches

Copyright 2013

ISBN: 978162-985002-3

Cover Design by Kristy Prince

DP
DECAPOLIS
PUBLISHING

A Club 52 Book

www.decapolisbooks.com

www.club52.com

Printed in the United States of America

TABLE OF CONTENTS

FOREWORD
BY DR. DAVE WILLIAMS

America's Pacesetting Life Coach™
Author of *Coming Into the Wealthy Place*

In 1994, Michael and Ramona Woods decided to take a risk. They saw a need for a multi-cultural hair care company to serve hair salons with high quality products, and to provide education on using those products with the latest hairstyle techniques. They took their mutual experience and passion for the salon industry and decided to fill a void in the marketplace.

The odds against them make this a modern David versus Goliath story. They began by mortgaging their home and sacrificing personal belongings to fund their company, which they named Ashtae after their two daughters Ashley and Taylore. Family, faith, and finances are pillars of their company's philosophy. I believe the Woods are successful because they started on the bottom, but they cared about their customers and that is what has taken them to the top.

Ashtae has grown tremendously. In 2009, they won the Wells Fargo Small Business of the Year Award. Ashtae products are now used in salons all over the United States, Canada, and the Caribbean Islands.

More importantly, the Woods see their company as a way to spread the Gospel. Selling hair care products serves as a vehicle to share the Word of God and finance its dissemination. And now they have launched a cutting edge television network, Black Network Television (BNT), featuring news, talk shows, sitcoms, and ministers from across America.

When I am with Michael and Ramona Woods, I receive an impartation. That is why I'm happy to endorse, affirm, and support them as they share their story and the underlying principles that led to their success and their entry into the wealthy place. The wealthy place is not only the way you think about financial matters, it is where you are living out God's will for your life.

By reading this book, you will receive an impartation of the truth and the spirit behind this powerful, humble couple. You will realize that God has given you the power to get wealth just as he has given Michael and Ramona the power to get wealth. The principles and experiences you discover in this book will help you understand how you, too, can come into the wealthy place.

May all the blessings God has poured out on the Woods be yours, as you put their wisdom into practice in your own life!

Thou hast caused men to ride over our heads; we went through fire and through water: but thou broughtest us out into a wealthy place.

Psalm 66:12 KJV

Michael and Ramona Woods with daughters, Ashley and Taylore.

CHAPTER 1

WAKE-UP!

Michael: Ramona and I were living in Buffalo, New York. We were newly married and had just begun to grow into our responsibilities as adults. One day I came home to find an extremely angry Ramona. As soon as I parked the car in the driveway she stormed out of the house, jumped into the car, and hollered, "Take me to the bank!"

Men, you know that when your wife is mad you don't get in her way. So I pulled the car out and we drove to the bank. She had this envelope in her hand and she kept saying, "How dare they! How dare they return my check?" The look in her eyes told me this was going to be a big day, for better or worse. I was hoping it was for better, since I was the husband trailing along behind hoping she didn't stir up too much trouble.

Before the car even stopped, Ramona opened the door and jumped out. She stormed into that bank as I followed meekly behind, bracing myself to intervene in case things got ugly. Once inside, I could hear her say to the teller, "I want to speak to a manager!" She was going straight to the top.

We hadn't started our company yet, and as a young couple we tried very hard to keep up with the Jones. As a result, we were destroying our credit. We wrote bad checks regularly, but usually they were to institutions, department stores, or other impersonal entities. This time a check to a friend had bounced, and Ramona felt humiliated. Our financial status was exposed. That was why she was so angry.

Little Incidents Often Uncover Big Problems

Not only that, the check that bounced was short just two dollars and thirty-nine cents. Sometimes when God is working on you, he allows little things to occur that reveal bigger problems in your life. That's what was happening before my eyes.

The bank tellers all knew who Ramona and I were because we were always bouncing checks, but this time a manager wasn't available. For a moment Ramona was stuck about what to do next. She demanded of the teller, "I want the bank to write a letter and tell this person the bank made a mistake. This shouldn't be my fault. I was only a couple of dollars short. You should have covered it! I want the bank to take the blame."

"I'm sorry, Mrs. Woods. I can't do that," the teller stated firmly.

"Then where's the manager?"

"The manager is unavailable to speak with you."

Upset and wanting a resolution in her favor, Ramona said to the young woman at the window, "Then I want all my money out of the bank. I'm going to close my account!"

Usually this bluff led to some sort of help or compromise about fees charged for overdrawing our account. But this day that is not what happened. The sweet young teller clicked on her keyboard and said, "Mrs. Woods, you have $227.00 in your account. I can help you close it right now. How would you like that $227.00, in twenties and ones?"

Our bank was letting us go! They didn't even want to fight for our patronage anymore. Something was really wrong. We were headed somewhere bad, fast.

A Turning Point

The steam went out of Ramona's anger. She had nothing left to say. She took the $227.00 and walked back to the car. That day would eventually come to be a major turning point for her and, in time, for me as well.

Ramona: I was totally irrational that day at the bank because my shame had been exposed. I wrote the bad check, not Michael. And it wasn't to a store but to someone I knew—someone I was trying to impress and build a reputation with. When you write a bad check to an institution, you really don't have any accountability. You can forget about it and shop somewhere else. But when you write it to an individual that you've been trying to impress, and then you get found out, it's crushing. Michael was trying to be supportive of me while keeping me out of trouble, but the full weight of this embarrassing episode came down on me. I went home and cried. This wasn't our first bad check by any means. But this time God shined a bright light on my behavior. He put a mirror in front of my face, and I did not like what I saw. Our financial situation was really bad!

Are You Ready?

Are you ready to live in the wealthy place? The first step you must take on this journey is found in the book of Romans, and it is the step I took that day.

Romans 13:11–14 NKJV

[11] And do this, knowing the time, that now it is high time to awake out of sleep; for now our salvation is nearer than when we first believed.

¹² The night is far spent, the day is at hand. Therefore let us cast off the works of darkness, and let us put on the armor of light.

¹³ Let us walk properly, as in the day, not in revelry and drunkenness, not in lewdness and lust, not in strife and envy.

¹⁴ But put on the Lord Jesus Christ, and make no provision for the flesh, to fulfill its lusts.

Notice that phrase, "awake out of sleep...."

W = Wake-Up

Friend, the first thing you have to do if you want to live in the wealthy place is simple but profound: Wake-up! You cannot afford to sleep anymore. You must wake-up to where you are and see what you are doing—for better or worse. Sometimes when God wakes you up, and you're not ready to be awakened, it is the toughest pill you will ever have to swallow. I swallowed that pill on the day the bank let us go. I said, "Lord, I don't know what you're trying to tell me here, but I am not going to continue to live my life this way."

That was my first step toward the wealthy place, and as badly as it hurt at the time, it was one of the best things that ever happened to me. Imagine how your life will change when you wake-up and catch a vision for living in the wealthy place—when you wake-up to a life with new habits, godly principles, and heavenly results. Here's the good news: You don't have to go through a difficult, embarrassing circumstance like we went through. God gives you the option of waking up on your own! It's always best to wake-up on your own. It is less painful. Think of waking up from natural sleep. It feels a whole lot better to wake-up on your own than to have someone shake you awake.

For years, we have gone upstairs each school day to wake-up our children. We call, "Get up out of bed. It's time to go to school." They groan and complain; they don't want to get up. It would be a lot more pleasant for them, and for us, if they woke up on their own. When our oldest daughter left for college, after her first week of classes, she called and said she had missed a class because she overslept. We weren't calling to awaken her anymore—she had to do it on her own. With freedom comes responsibility.

The same is true of you. You can either take the responsibility to wake yourself up; or God will orchestrate a situation in your life that will wake you up. It might not happen in a pleasant way, like my wake-up call, but he wants you to go to the wealthy place!

We have lived through many "wake-up" periods in our life while growing the company, and in our marketplace ministry. We constantly grow in what God wants us to do. All of us go through wake-up stages on the path to the wealthy place. The day the bank stood up to me was one of the best days of my life, because after I wrote that bad check we *never* wrote another one. Thanks be to God!

Collections Calling

At that time, our credit was so bad we were constantly getting calls from creditors and collection agencies.[1] Michael would get ugly with them on the phone. He would say, "I know I owe you money! I will pay you when I have it to give." If they upset him, he would say, "If you make me mad, I'll put you at the bottom of the will-pay list!"

But after that check bounced, I quietly began tackling our credit problems. I didn't ask Michael to join me because he did not have the desire to change yet. He did not recognize that our bad credit was a problem. I never told Michael, "Okay, now you've got to change." I just dealt with the things I knew were not straight. I looked at our credit as a couple; I looked at his, I looked at mine and systematically dealt with each problem I found. At that time,

---

[1] Proverbs 22:7 NLT

God was dealing with me. Michael's spending habits were way too much for me to deal with, but God gave me grace to go after mine first.

Tackling Debt

So I began tackling the debt bit by bit. It wasn't long before Michael came into alignment with God's way of looking at finances. He no longer yelled at creditors on the phone when they called. Instead he promised he would pay them slowly but surely. When you are heading in the right direction, you have peace in your situation even if it takes a while to climb out of the hole you dug for yourself. And we suddenly had peace. Little did we know that one day we would build a million-dollar company and realize so many spiritual, financial, and family dreams! At least for me, I am convinced that it started that day at the bank.

This is Your Moment

Friend, wake-up! Wake yourself up before God awakens you. If you are putting up a front in your financial situation just to maintain a reputation with others, then you are living in deception. Maybe you avoid certain people because you wrote a bad check. Maybe you behave dishonorably toward institutions who lent you money in good faith. Even if your spouse isn't ready to wake-up, you can! People wake-up at different times and for different reasons. But you can decide right now that this is your miracle moment. Don't wait for the hammer to come down.

The first letter in wealthy is "W," which stands for Wake-up! Wake-up and start moving to the wealthy place!

"And you shall remember the Lord your God, for it is He who gives you power to get wealth, that He may establish His covenant which He swore to your fathers, as it is this day."

Deuteronomy 8:18 NKJV

Michael and Ramona relating the story of their Hawaiian SCUBA diving adventure at the Dave Williams' Wealthy Place Seminar in Rochester, Michigan.

2
CHAPTER

GET EDUCATED

The second letter in the word wealthy is "E." Waking up is the first step to take on your journey to the wealthy place. The second step to the wealthy place is education.

E = Education

You may wake-up to your situation, but if you don't seek proper instruction on how to make the changes you need to make, you won't move toward the wealthy place. Ignoring instruction will ensure that you stay stuck right where you are. [1]

Michael: I learned this the hard way on a trip to Hawaii we took as a newly married couple. Ramona and I decided to do something crazy: we went scuba diving. It involved taking a class in the morning and then going for a dive after that. I have to tell you a secret. At that time my wife couldn't swim very well. I could only swim a little bit better, so I thought maybe I didn't have to listen as closely to what the instructor said because at least I could keep myself afloat.

---

[1] 2 Timothy 2:15 NLT; Proverbs 13:18 KJV

We went to a pool to learn how to scuba dive and the instructor took us through the steps. Ramona was paying close attention but I was thinking, *I can swim a little bit, so just teach my wife.* I didn't pay attention to the instructor because I thought I had it together.

Soon we walked out to the beach wearing all our gear and kept on walking right into the Pacific Ocean. The gear felt a lot heavier as I walked than it had in the pool. We put on our masks and fins and everything else, and as soon as we got in the water I noticed that my wife was moving around a lot better than I was. In fact, while I lagged behind, Ramona and the instructor were flapping away. And they were holding hands. Ramona was afraid enough of the ocean and had a good estimate of her abilities, so she was sticking close to the instructor.

I watched them swim deeper and deeper, holding hands. I thought, *okay, I'm going to catch up with them.* I followed them down and it was beautiful along the way. I saw all types of fish: blue, red, orange, and yellow. The only kind of fish I had seen before were trout, and they were fried and sitting on a plate. Finally I caught up with them and we spent some time together on the ocean floor. The instructor took a picture of us. After a while he signaled, *are you ready to go up?* We nodded yes. I was still looking around because I was amazed at the beauty surrounding me. Suddenly, I noticed I was alone!

Panic: The Price of Not Listening

I had been waiting for us to go up together, but now I didn't see my wife or the instructor. As I peered up through the water I could barely see four fins flapping away. I thought *I know they didn't just leave me*—but they had! I began scrambling and went into the "I'm going to get out of here fast!" mode. I started flapping my fins, but I couldn't remember what the instructor had said about how to go up.

As much as I flapped, I wasn't moving. I panicked. Forgetting whatever instruction I had received back in the pool, I now employed my own technique, using movements the instructor never mentioned. It basically involved kicking my fins as hard as I could, and grabbing at the water with my hands and arms until I somehow started to go up. Little by little, with great effort, I moved upward. Finally I saw I was close. With a last, awkward burst of flapping I broke the surface of the water and threw myself on the boat, gasping.

Ramona and the instructor were sitting there pleasantly talking while I was feeling like I had just dodged death. I thought to myself, *I'm never going scuba diving again!*

Of course the problem wasn't scuba diving or the instructor. The problem was that I had totally ignored the instruction and had paid the price in panic. Ramona recognized that we had a mentor in the pool who had done this a thousand times. She chose to listen to the mentor and did not deviate from his instructions. Like many people, I only half-listened. That day I realized that I didn't have it all together all the time. Had I just listened, I would have been safer and enjoyed the experience a lot more. I could have gone scuba diving with Ramona, rather than watching from behind as the instructor held hands with her!

Going Where You've Never Gone

When you are trying to go to a place that you've never gone before, like the wealthy place, you need to seek out the right instruction—and then pay attention to it! From that day forward, I paid attention whenever someone was giving me instruction. I didn't want to get stuck at the bottom of the sea again!

Mentors Are Treasures

Educated people make good decisions. If you stop learning, you stop earning. Education is vital—not optional—for your

23

success. You have to stay sharp. One of the best ways to do this is to seek out mentors. Mentorship plays a big part in our development. We have several mentors; some of them are billionaires who own major companies. You don't need people at the highest levels all the time, but you do need someone who is doing better than you are to help you get where you want to be.

It is important to understand how a mentor thinks, not just what he or she does. A good mentor will teach you how to think for success. Ramona and I have mentors in spiritual, business, finances, and personal areas of our lives. Each of them is a specialist in their own area of expertise. You wouldn't necessarily go to your pastor for advice on building a company, any more than you would go to a CEO for deep spiritual advice. Go to people who are gifted in the area in which you need to grow.

Honor Your Mentors

It takes patience to mentor, so honor your mentors for their service to you. One mentor looked at our business and said, "I'm not used to dealing with such small numbers." It was a sacrifice for him to help us. Honor your mentors by paying whenever you go out for a meal with them. Give them gifts when appropriate, and thank them for sowing their time and interest into your life.

Getting instruction from wise friends and mentors has made the difference in our lives, our business, and our ministry together. Our mentors never simply give us the answer, but they provide an invaluable sounding board which helps us find our way to the answer. We are energized being around people who are excited and energized and have found the wealthy place. I love watching a visionary who is making things happen.

Who are the people you go to for decisions for business, marriage and family, and spiritual advice? Do you have a diverse group of people giving you advice in their areas of specialty?

Education will make or break you in your path toward the wealthy place.

- W = Wake-up!
- E = Education

Now let's move on to the third principle that is contained in the word wealthy: A = Attitude.

Your attitude is the determining factor of how quickly you move ahead.

CHAPTER

CHANGE YOUR ATTITUDE

Ramona: Sometimes it's easy to look only at the negatives—especially when there do not seem to be any positives. That was my attitude on the day I had almost given up on all we were working for. It was the day God confronted me at the welfare office.

Michael and I had been in business for three or four years and we were losing everything. There are many expenses involved in starting a company, especially when you're dealing with products and inventory. We were spending a lot to get started, but not making nearly enough to sustain the business or even pay our basic bills. Our cars were already repossessed, we had received a foreclosure notice on our house, and we were in debt over $470,000.00. Michael was out working hard every day, driving around in a beat-up van full of our hair care products. I worked the business from home and also took care of our daughters, who were three years old and eighteen months old at the time.

When You Lose Hope

Nothing seemed to be moving us forward, and I finally reached an all-time low. I decided to take measures into my own hands. I had lost hope, and when you lose hope, fear has a way of attacking you. I was at that place of fear. I felt that my attitude was justified. I was upset with everybody. I was scared. I took a city bus with the two girls to a building downtown. I had never been there before. The lady at the window was rude and said, "Take a number." Taylore and Ashley didn't know where we were, but I did. It was the welfare office in Greensboro. It was an ugly, fearful, impolite place, and I had gone there voluntarily, driven by fear.

I took a number and sat in the waiting room. I didn't know the system. I heard numbers being called. My girls thought it was fun and they played at my feet, but I was doing my best to not cry. I didn't want my kids to see me crying or to know that we were in a place that brought me shame. As I held back tears I thought, how did I end up here? How has this happened to us?

I sat there for a long time. The world around me seemed to disappear. I just kept asking myself, *Ramona, what are you doing here?*

The Difference between "State" and "Fate"

At some point they called our number because Taylore said, "Mommy, that's our number!" She thought we were at Disneyland or something, and was so excited she kept pulling on me saying, "Mommy, Mommy. Our number! They called our number." But right when they called my number, the Holy Spirit convicted me and asked me a question that I'll never forget. He said, "Ramona, is this your state, or is this your fate?" I ran that question through my head again. Was this my fate—my permanent direction—or my state—a temporary place on the way somewhere else? He then said, "If this is your fate, you need to stay here. Present your number and accept the welfare. But if this is just a state in time, a period in your life that you can learn from, then get yourself up and walk out of here and go back to work." I stood up. I grabbed my daughters and said, "Come on." I walked out of there, wiped my tears, threw my number away, got on the bus, sat down and said, "This is just a state, a point in my life. It's not forever." I went back to our foreclosed house, which we were still living in and trying to make payments on, but my attitude was changed. I started shouting because I was so grateful. "Lord, thank you! Thank you that we haven't sunk yet. Thank you that this tough time is not permanent but just a passing period. Thank you that a friend lent us money so we can stay in this house and maybe avoid foreclosure. Thank you for my children and my husband and our health. Thank you!" Then, out of sheer gratitude, I began to sing along with a praise song on the radio. I turned the song up loud and every bit of fear vanished.

I went into our little office, a converted bedroom, got on the phone and called a customer. "Good morning, Mrs. Jones! How are you today? This is Ramona with Ashtae products. Let me tell you about today's special." And on I went with my sales pitch. She said, "I'll take it." "Great, Mrs. Jones." You'll receive it in two days."

The Soil for Success

I made another phone call and made another sale. I became relentless and hopeful. Our situation had not changed—we still owed the same amount of money and still faced the same obstacles—but my attitude had changed, and that became the soil for success. It wasn't just a positive "I can do it" attitude, but a thankful attitude—I was thankful to the Lord from whom all provision and blessing flows.

A = Attitude: Find Your Gratitude

The "A" in wealthy stands for attitude. Your attitude is the determining factor of how quickly you move ahead.[1] When you are down low it is hard to express gratitude, but that is when

---

[1] Ephesians 4:23 AMP

God wants to hear it most! Lack of money is never a good reason to be ungrateful. Once I learned that, I was set free. From that point on, every time we won a new customer, whether she spent fifty dollars or a thousand dollars, I would say to God, "Thank you." To this day we send every customer something on his or her birthday. For every stylist who has a death in the family, we send a hundred dollars to help with funeral arrangements. Every customer who is going through a difficult time receives free products for a month. Maybe our generosity will inspire gratitude in them and they will learn to give God thanks, just as God had taught me that day.

If you're in what appears to be a hopeless situation, I challenge you to find your gratitude. Don't worry anymore about what other people think about you.[1] Find a song and rejoice. Look around you and thank God for every little thing. Because when it's all said and done, the things that matter most are family and health. A lot of times we go around muttering about our woes. "Oh, they laid me off," you tell your cousins. "They laid me off," you tell your friends. When something like this happens, you must say, "Thank you, Lord, for this change in my situation. Thank you for giving me this opportunity. I know they think they laid me off, but you just gave me time to meditate on what you really want me to do. I was only working there because that was where I was supposed to be for a season. Now I'm ready to go into the wealthy place. I'm glad they let me go from bondage." Count it all joy![2]

It's time for you to wake-up, get energized, and get ready to move to the wealthy place. That "bad break" is just what you needed to get you moving. You were sitting in the wrong place too long, just like I was sitting in the wrong place

---

[1] Proverbs 29:25 AMP

[2] James 1:2–4 NLT

at the welfare office. Turn it around. Move forward. The bigger question is, "What are you going to do next?" Lack of money is never a reason to go through depression or a down attitude. Instead, see it as a perfect time to try something else! Since the day when God taught me the true meaning of gratitude, I check my attitude all the time. That experience changed my life forever. When you change your attitude, it's powerful. Nobody's going to turn your gratitude switch on for you. You need to recognize when you are ungrateful. It has to click inside you. Then you can repent for being ungrateful and get back on your journey to the wealthy place.

Keep moving forward!

- W = Wake-up!
- E = Education
- A = Attitude

Next, we'll investigate the "L" in wealthy.

To get to a new place, you have to leave old places and old baggage behind.

CH A P T E R

LEAVE!

Michael: You've awakened, become educated, and changed your attitude. The next letter is "L" and that stands for leave. That's right—leave! The people of Israel had to leave Egypt to get to the Promised Land. You had to leave your parents to go out on your own, or to get married.[1] We all had to leave childhood to become adults.[2] Life is about leaving certain places so we can arrive at new ones. It's about leaving the past so we can come into the wealthy place.

Philippians 3:13–14 KJV

[13] Brethren, I count not myself to have apprehended: but this one thing I do, forgetting those things which are behind, and reaching forth unto those things which are before,

[14] I press toward the mark for the prize of the high calling of God in Christ Jesus.

---

[1] Matthew 19:5 KJV

[2] 1 Corinthians 13:11 KJV

Familiar vs. Uncertain

When you go on a "God Journey," you may not know how you're going to get there. You may not know what you're going to do between Egypt and the Promised Land. You won't always feel comfortable between your "now" and your "future." Leaving is difficult because you let go of what's familiar to embrace an uncertain future. There are some things—and even some people—that you must leave behind if you want to arrive at the wealthy place.

Leaving is tough. As you leave, you may feel like you're out there all by yourself. All you have is your faith in God. All you have is that moment in time when you asked yourself, "What's going to happen next?"

Many times we don't want to go through the leaving process. We want to instantly arrive! But that's not how it works. To get to a new place, you have to leave old places and old baggage behind. Otherwise, you carry too much. It's like flying. When you travel on small airplanes, they weigh everything to make sure too much baggage doesn't weigh down the plane. It makes me nervous to see people trying to board a small plane with four bags. I want to say, "This is not a shopping excursion! Don't weigh down this plane with that excess luggage." That's how it is on the way to the wealthy place.

Red Roof Inn or The Plaza?

Perhaps the most difficult thing to leave behind is our poverty mentality. Ramona and I, by simple statistics, should not be where we are today. When I consider our journey and all we've been through, I am amazed. We are not the smartest people in the world. Neither of us has a bachelor's degree. We know that God is in this because there's no other way it could have happened. Yet we have had to leave behind our own "stinking thinking"[3] in order to have blessings poured on us.

---

[3] Romans 12:1–2 AMP; Ephesians 4:23 AMP

I recall a time early in the business when our family was more accustomed to staying at the Red Roof Inn than at a first class hotel. As a matter of fact, we had never even seen a luxury hotel until we traveled with our daughters to New York City on business. Just for fun, I brought them to see The Plaza hotel. My daughter liked what she saw and told me, "Daddy, we should stay here!" At that time, The Plaza was not in our budget. We could barely afford to get to New York! But her words got into my spirit and challenged me.[4] When I told her we couldn't afford such a nice hotel she replied, "Daddy, why can't we afford it?" Her question stuck with me, and a change of mind took place in me that day. I told the family, "We are staying in The Plaza, even if it takes every last penny we have right now."

And we did. That night we felt like royalty. The girls pranced around the room in hotel robes. We couldn't afford to go to one of the hotel restaurants, so we found a little restaurant nearby that sold chicken, rice, and frijoles. We got it to go and walked into The Plaza with our bags of food.

Once you are exposed to excellence, you never want to go back. The Red Roof Inn would never be good enough for our family again. We had experienced The Plaza!

Discomfort...At First

Leaving makes you feel uncomfortable at first. I remember the first time I went to New York and gawked at all the tall buildings. I remember the first time I saw a million-dollar home. I'm from the country and had never seen such a thing. I remember the first time I was on a yacht.

To get to the wealthy place, you have to be willing to leave the places, the standards, the ideas, and even the people you embraced before.

---

[4] Proverbs 18:21 KJV

Time Out

There is another sense in which we sometimes have to leave, and that's when we need a rest. There are times when God will call you to leave your present situation and take a time out. He did this with his own disciples. A "time out" is where you stop because you physically need rest. Life is so full that sometimes you require a break; you will find that during your time out, your creativity will kick in again.

Sometimes God puts you in a time out, just as a parent does with a misbehaving child, because you're not allowing God to work but are trying to do it all by yourself. Sometimes you find yourself in a time out situation without wanting to be there. But other times it's just a temporary break, meant to recharge your creativity, hope, and energy. When you're resting, God can speak to you. When you're busy, it's almost impossible to hear God's voice clearly. My greatest thoughts have come at 5:45 in the morning; sometimes I can't find a pen fast enough to write the ideas down. They come when I'm resting or sleeping rather than when I'm running around like a mad man, doing, doing, and doing.

When you are resting, you can reflect on what is working, what is not working, and what tough decisions you need to make. This is when God's plan becomes clear to your heart.

I make sure to rest before I begin praying specifically for our future. When I have something specific to pray about—like a job, a new idea for our business, or a new ministry to support—I rest, pray, and then I take action.

But it's difficult to get to the point of taking action when you haven't rested and thought about it and waited to hear from the Lord. When you're physically exhausted, it's harder to hear the Holy Spirit. So give yourself a time out. When everything is falling apart in front of you, the hardest thing to do is to take time away. You have to ask, "Am I wearing too many hats? Am I being effective? Am I getting the most out of what I have obligated myself to do? Am I running out of ideas?"

Leave the playing field for a little while. Let God speak to you in the resting time.[5] Leave behind those things that are not taking you to the wealthy place—expectations and standards, ideas, habits, friendships, or beliefs. Only when you leave these things behind can you follow God to where he is taking you next.

Matthew 11:28–29 KJV

[28] Come unto me, all ye that labour and are heavy laden, and I will give you rest.

[29] Take my yoke upon you, and learn of me; for I am meek and lowly in heart: and ye shall find rest unto your souls.

---

[5] Mark 6:31 KJV; Hebrews 4:3–5 KJV

You cannot be wealthy or successful without self-control.

CHAPTER

GET TRANSFORMED!

Michael: After leaving behind the things that are keeping you from moving forward, it's time to take the next step on your journey to the wealthy place. The "T" in wealthy stands for transformation. This Bible passage speaks directly to the idea of transforming your mind to conform to God's way of living:

> **Romans 12:2 NKJV**
> "And do not be conformed to this world, but be transformed by the renewing of your mind, that you may prove what is that good and acceptable and perfect will of God."

We have addressed Ramona's times of transformation. Now it's time to look at mine.

To get to the wealthy place a transformation must happen, and it happens at different stages for different people. You may not anticipate when God decides it's time for you to transform. Earlier, Ramona had her transformational breakthrough when she wrote a check to a friend that bounced. That woke her up to the necessity of getting our finances in order. Then she was challenged again when she went to the welfare office to apply for welfare, while I was out working day and night trying to provide for my family. That's a terrible feeling for a husband, and she didn't tell me what she had done until four or five years later. But that's where we were emotionally and financially at the time. She had lost hope, but God transformed her thinking in an instant.

God Gets My Attention

My transformational situations came after Ramona's. They lit a fire under me and caused me to say, "I want to be in a wealthy place, because I cannot go through this again."

The first life-transforming event happened when both of my daughters were in private school. My youngest daughter, Ashley, was in preschool and Taylore was in grade school; it was very expensive, $12,000 a year. The school they attended kept calling because we had not paid our tuition bill.

Ring, ring, ring. "I won't answer that," I would say. I avoided them every time. Ring, ring, ring. "Nope, don't answer that call, either." They sent letters because we had not paid our bill, but I ignored those as well. Finally, one day I went to pick up Ashley, I saw her standing in the line of kids waiting to be picked up by their parents. Pinned to her shirt with a big safety pin was a letter. I knew what it was, and I thought, *They did not just do this to my baby girl.* I could feel my blood pressure surging.

My heart hurt on that drive home. The Lord and I had a talk. I said, "Lord, you know I'm working every day, trying to be a good husband and father, trying to provide for my family. Why do I have to go through this? Why?" The Lord had an answer, but it would take me a while to hear it.

We ended up having to pull both girls out of private school and putting them in public school for the next three years. It was a tough thing for us. As a man, I felt I was not able to supply the needs of my family. It seemed like I was getting a private lesson from God because I had not heeded the lesson he taught Ramona when she got her wake-up call at the bank. He was going to take me through some challenging situations to reset my thinking so I could get to another place. He will do the same thing to you.

Losing the Loan

The second transformational event occurred when we applied for a loan from the bank. Our business moved slowly forward, but it wasn't fast enough. We struggled to maintain our cash flow, so we applied for a $25,000 loan. At first, the bank was very positive. They told me we would likely get the loan, and I arranged to fly to New York to sign the paperwork.

At this time in our business, we had family members working for the company but there was no accountability. Ramona had pinpointed the problem already, but I was trying to avoid it. Instead, I wanted to fix that problem with this loan that would give us a much needed infusion of cash. When we found out, unofficially, that we were going to get the loan, we began to spend that money to cover costs we had incurred.

I arrived at the bank office in New York and met with Bob and Mary, the loan officers. "You're doing a good job with your company," Bob said, but after saying a few more nice things he started using words I didn't like—such as "however" and "but." Finally he came to the bottom line and said, "However, I'm sorry but we are unable to give you this loan."

His words were so unexpected that at first I didn't take them in. I said to myself, *he didn't just say that we did not get this loan; certainly I misunderstood.* As his words and the bank's decision sunk in, I felt myself getting hot. We had already spent that money. It was one of the worst feelings I have ever experienced.

"Then what should I do?" I demanded. "You said we were getting this loan!" His words stabbed my heart: "Mr. Woods, it's your business. You must turn it around." I got up from the chair and said, "Bob, we're not going to let this stop us. We'll make it. You'll see."

I walked down a long hallway that connected the bank to a nearby mall. I had a client in that mall. During that long walk I heard God speak to my heart in a way I had never heard before—or at least I hadn't listened to before. Now I had nowhere else to go. "You thought the bank was going to come through for you, didn't you?" The Lord asked me. "You depended on them. Who are you going to depend on now?"

It was a cold, lonely walk. All the while my pager was beeping. Ramona wanted to know if the loan would come in the form of a check, a bank transfer, or what. She needed to make payroll. She didn't know we hadn't gotten the loan at all, and our business was in danger of collapsing. Instead of answering her page and calling her back, I decided to do something else. I went to visit our client in the mall.

I went into that salon and said, "Hey, Debbie, how are you doing?" I started shaking containers. "You're out of the Ashtae clarifying shampoo that removes oil from the hair. You need some Ashtae conditioner to moisturize those clients' hair. You need some Ashtae color, some cool sensation dandruff shampoo." I shook all the containers and sold her $500 worth of product. Did she need those products? No! But I needed the money.

Then I drove down to Katie's salon and got $400 in sales from Katie. I went all over Rochester and got all sorts of orders. Ramona kept on paging, but when I called the orders in I wouldn't spend any more time on the phone with her than I needed to. I'd give her the order and get right off, ignoring her questions about the loan.

At 11 p.m. I was still visiting salons. When I would see a light on in the back I would knock and say, "I know you're in there. Open up!" The salon owners didn't need to see me at that time of night, but I needed to see them. When you're relentless you just keep moving. In my mind I had just lost $25,000, so I didn't care if the lights were out. I'd go to the back door or the side door and knock until someone answered.

Building the Business Properly

God transformed my mind that day. He took my reliance off the loan and put it where it needed to be: building our business God's way.[1]

> **Romans 12:11 NLT**
> Never be lazy, but work hard and serve the Lord enthusiastically.

> **1 Thessalonians 4:11 CEV**
> Try your best to live quietly, to mind your own business, and to work hard, just as we taught you to do.

One part of that was bringing accountability to our employees. God revealed all the waste I had been tolerating. We didn't know it, but we were hiring for the wrong reasons. We felt good about hiring people because it made us feel good: "We hired five new people! Yes, she works for me, and she works for me. I've got it going on." Whether they did any work at all didn't matter as much. It was mismanagement and God was calling us to account. He wasn't giving us an easy way out. He wanted us to go to the wealthy place, and I needed to transform my thinking first.

Refocusing for a Better Future

I got back to North Carolina, and Ramona and I spent our last few hundred dollars on the most powerful tool that any business can have: a time clock. When we installed that time clock, every single employee quit the same day. The company was two-and-a-

---

[1] Proverbs 22:29 KJV

half years old. Our debt was $470,000. We had bad credit. Our home was in foreclosure. Every car was repossessed. Ramona was taking the bus with the kids to get around. But God refocused and transformed us to prepare us for a better future.

When everyone quit, it was a very humbling time for us. But it was perhaps the best thing that ever happened to me because I realized I was accountable for everything concerning the business. Bob's words were a revelation to me: "It's your business. You turn it around." That was the day Ramona and I got on the same page. We knew the solution was within us, not outside of us. We were running an unaccountable business. From then on we made everyone accountable to the vision, and it changed everything.

You cannot be wealthy or successful without self-control.[2]

Proverbs 5:23 CEV
They get lost and die because of their foolishness and lack of self-control.

Proverbs 25:28 NLT
A person without self-control is like a city with broken-down walls.

You have to control your thoughts, your money, and your time. When you control yourself, you move forward faster. You stay focused on the goal without being distracted. You do what you say. You open the store when your hours say you will, whether or not there are customers. And you hold everyone—including yourself—accountable.

Once major transformation happens and you see what can be, there is no going back. Your better future starts to burn inside of you. Ideas begin to flow.

---

[2] 1 Timothy 3:2 NLT

You have been transformed! Now let's review our journey so far:

- W = Wake-up!
- E = Educate
- A = Attitude
- L = Leave your old place
- T = Transformed

Next we'll explore the "H" in wealthy.

Challenging situations should cause us to hearken to God's voice.

CHAPTER

HEARKEN!

Michael: That brings us to the letter "H" in wealthy: H = "hearken." To hearken means to hear with the intention of taking action. Many people listen to a pastor or instructor and think they hear the message, but they don't actually hearken to it. They don't listen with the intention of making a move. Many times the people closest to the pastor or leader aren't experiencing the wealthy place. They are too close. They're hearing the same thing over and over but not hearkening to the message.

Take Heed to What You Hear

You must be careful to whom you hearken. When you begin to move toward the wealthy place and are on that journey, you will find yourself surrounded by many people, some of them with negative thinking or gossip on their minds. They don't want to go to the wealthy place, and they want to keep *you* from going. The longer you listen, the more likely you are to hearken to their destructive words.

Mark 4:24 CEV
Listen carefully to what you hear! The way you treat others
will be the way you will be treated—and even worse.

When people spout garbage, don't volunteer to be their trash
can. If you're on the hearing or receiving end of bad ideas and
gossip, you are serving as a trash can. You've got to move forward.
Hearkening to the wrong stuff will keep you in bondage.

Hearkening to the Word of God keeps you grounded. When
you are in the flesh, you are concerned about what the world
thinks about you, and you listen to the world. When you are in
the spirit, you hearken to God. You are moved by his Word. If
CNN, FOX, NBC, and CBS are more interesting than GOD,
you are in the world.

Many people sit in front of the television set and let the news
tell them what to believe. They hearken to the news: "What happened? What's the latest story? What's the update?" They get
wrapped up in things they shouldn't waste time on. Instead they
should say, "Let me get into the Word and see what the Word
says, because I know the Word will keep me protected and going
in the right direction. I only hearken to God's words."

1 John 2:15 NLT
Do not love this world nor the things it offers you, for when
you love the world, you do not have the love of the Father
in you.

You, the Entrepreneur

Some people hit a rough patch and hearken to despair. They
get fired or laid off and think it's the end of the world. Says who?
Your former boss? Sure, maybe you lost your job. Don't have a
pity party about it. God is telling you through your circumstance
that there is an entrepreneur inside of you waiting to get out.
Your employer saw it before you did, that's all.

Some people hearken to their title or position. Be cautious and don't feel so high and mighty. We do not have titles at our company. Everyone has the same title: WORK. We do things cooperatively at the office. If the bathroom needs to be cleaned, we do it. That brings out the best in all of us. When we hire people, we hire them to work.

Challenging situations should cause us to hearken to God's voice.[1] Listen to what God says and begin to change your mind. If you need more education, get more education. If you need to get with a group of people who are going after the wealthy place, then do it. Start a business. Start baking cakes. Start detailing cars. Go back to school. Sharpen your saw. Yes, there are going to be changes. We know what it's like when the bank tells you, "No, you can't grow your vision." We know what those challenges are. But you must keep on hearkening to God. Sit down and pray for your family, pray for your kids, pray for each other. Hearken unto the Word, not to the economy and not to the bad advice you may be getting from those around you.

Just One Idea

When you get together with someone, you should not pray about the recession, but you should pray that God gives you an idea. Just one idea is all you need to set things on fire. Don't get caught up in the flesh, because the flesh complains. When you are in the flesh, you are easily offended. When you're in the Spirit, you don't even realize an offense occurred.

Hearken to Success

Success begins with hearkening to the right voices. Early in our business we decided we didn't want our company to just be a local enterprise, so we sought clients in many states. Then we

---

[1] Psalm 29:3 NLT; Jeremiah 33:3 KJV

took a really big risk. It took every penny we had to participate in the biggest trade show in New York City. The cost just to be in the show was $42,000. The major players in hair care were there. They put $200,000 into making their booths look fancy. We had to be creative and make our displays by hand. We didn't have great graphics. It took everything we had to just have a presence at the event.

We soon realized that nobody knew who we were—and nobody much cared. Customers at the show would come by and ask, "Ash-what?" They couldn't pronounce the name and had never heard of our products. Our goal was to sell products, but everyone we talked to said, "I've never heard of Ashtae." Customers don't want to buy something that no one else is buying, so no one was buying Ashtae.

Ramona: I was saying, "Oh, God, what are we going to do?" My heart was thumping; my calculator mind was whirling because we had planted everything into this.

But Michael is the most creative guy. He gathered everybody on our sales team. We were scared. We had zero sales the first day. Michael stood before us and said the opposite of what we had been hearing: "Don't you know that everyone has heard of Ashtae? This is what you're going to do. When someone says, 'I've never heard of Ashtae,' you say, 'You've never heard of Ashtae! Where have you been? Everybody's using Ashtae!'" He had us practice those lines. Every person on our team had to get up in front and practice saying, "You've never heard of Ashtae?"

I'm telling you, the next day the Holy Spirit came into that booth. The amazing thing that happened was a stylist came by and said, "I've never heard of Ashtae." Before we could give our new found pitch, another woman standing at the booth said, "I use Ashtae. I've been using it for years." I almost said, "You do?" but the Holy Spirit prompted me to just shut up. The rest is history. We started selling Ashtae like you wouldn't believe and made almost all our money back that week, and we won many new clients as well.

We hearkened to the right voice, not the wrong one. You can, too. Turn off the wrong voices. Don't hearken to doubt and despair—God has a better place for you to go.

It's called the wealthy place!

What do you do when you are in the midst of challenges and valleys? We'll deal with those next.

We're all prone to be more selfish, self-focused, and prideful on the peak because we seem to have no cares; we like to think it's because we're so smart.

7

TOUGH MOMENTS ON
THE JOURNEY: SAY YES!

Michael: Sometimes we say to each other, "What is God trying to do? I don't understand this situation!" We all go through tough times. That's the point where you must say "Yes!" to God and to his will. The "Y" in wealthy place = Yes.

It's easy to say "yes" to God when you are doing well, enjoying a high point. When you're on a peak, you're up high and nothing can bring you down. Everything seems to be working. You seem to be on the same page as God. Life is beautiful.

When You Come Off the Peak

But you can't stay on the peak all the time. For one thing, it would wear you out. Ramona works out every day. Sometimes it's annoying how committed she is to it. Once I visited her workout place to see what it was all about. What was getting my wife up every morning at 5:00 a.m.? What was the big deal? It was a spinning (stationary bike) class, and I was the only guy there. I got on a bike in the back so that if I fell off nobody would notice. The seats were really small and it was nothing like riding a bike. The women were gung-ho. The leader of the class said, "We're going to start slow and get into our 'yellow' zone." I thought; I can do this. But soon I was panting. The instructor talked to us as if we were traveling together: "Mary, now it's your turn to lead us up the mountain." Then it was someone else's turn, and then it was my turn. I about died! I was so thankful when the class was over, and I vowed I would *never* go back.

Spinning that day was like being on a peak. You cannot remain on a peak forever. It can kill you. You can only sustain that level of outpouring of energy for a while. Then you have to come down.

There are certain dangers to living on the peak as well. When we're on a peak, we have found that our old natures assert themselves more than when we are in a valley. We're all prone to be more selfish, self-focused, and prideful on the peak because we seem to have no cares; we like to think it's because we're so smart. Everything is going our way. It's easy to forget God when everything is going our way. The valley brings us back to earth and humbles us—which is a good thing. It reminds us that we need each other, that we need God's wisdom, that our success isn't only the result of our own efforts. We have observed that more divorces happen at the peak than in the valley. Why? People don't have the money to get a divorce when they are in the valley. They can't afford to divide their strength. Being in the valley encourages couples to stay together and, in the long run, they are thankful for that.

The Long Drive

Still, it can be difficult to say yes to God in the valley. I'll never forget when we bought the big building we are in now. We closed on the purchase in April, and almost instantly everything around us seemed to fall apart. The U.S. economy went into a nosedive, and so the lessees we had lined up to fill the building vanished.

Every single tenant who was going to rent part of the facility left. That didn't concern me much because we always relied on God. We said, "We'll get some new tenants. That's just small stuff. God is going to provide." We kept saying yes to God.

Then my twenty-five year old niece died and I spoke at her funeral. Her loss really hurt, but I kept saying yes to God. Within months my brother-in-law died. Again I had to comfort my sister and stand in front of the people believing that God is who he says he is. Again, I said "yes" to God.

Two months later my brother died. Three months after that, my other brother died. Now my "yes" to God turned into a bunch of questions. "Lord, come on. When is enough, enough? I'm believing even while I'm doing funeral after funeral, but this is getting hard." I am the youngest of nine children, and in my family I'm always the one up front giving encouragement to everybody. I kept saying yes to God, but all the time I could feel the weight getting heavier.

Lord, It's Too Much

Finally, after the last funeral, I got in the car and told Ramona, "I have to go for a drive." I'm not a really emotional person, but at that moment I needed to get away for a bit and get a hold on God. I got in that car, turned the music on, and drove. I was feeling so low, like the Lord had put too much on me. Sometimes we feel like he has put too much on us to carry. I was asking him, "Why? Why? Why?"

I remembered a line from a Psalm my mother used to recite to me when I was a boy:

Psalm 23:4 NKJV
Yea, though I walk through the valley of the shadow of death, I will fear no evil; for You are with me; Your rod and Your staff, they comfort me.

I thought back to my mom, who had passed away due to a stroke when I was just nine years old. I remembered her kissing me goodbye as I went off to school that day, and when I came home my sisters and brothers said she was in the hospital. I waited for her to come home, but was soon told she didn't make it. As a child, I didn't understand what the words really meant until they said she had died. The feeling of loneliness was so overpowering that I stopped talking to everyone for several days. Questions ran through my head, "Who is going to take care of me and my older brother? Who will greet me when I come home from school? Where will we live? Who will love us like Momma did?" I thank God to this day that my sister, Connie, and my older brothers and sisters were there to answer many of those questions and bring me comfort in my lonely state of mind.

Now I was feeling a similar loneliness. But I was starting to see why Momma had clung to Psalm 23 so much. She had gone through her own trials I am sure, and I knew there were times when she found it hard to say yes to God. The true test is believing that the Word of God will take you through every worldly trial and keep you moving forward.

Five hours later I was in Atlanta, but I still did not feel relief. I had decided to drive until I heard from God again. Finally, hours after I had begun, I heard God speaking to me. He took me back in my mind to my high school days and said, "Yes, terrible things are happening all around you, but in each instance it could've been you. Do you remember when you were playing on the playground with those guys and one of your friends got shot over a game of basketball? That could have been you. Do you remember when you were in a car accident when your mother was driving, and you all were thrown across the railroad tracks? You were thrown out of the back seat, but there wasn't a scratch on you. You could have died that day. Do you remember when you and your future wife were in a club in London, England, and shots broke out, and you swept her off her feet and ran out of the place? It could have been you."

He showed me how many times he had preserved my life. At that point I had my answer. I turned the car around. God continued to talk to me: "I'm not finished with you yet. I've got great works for you to do." It was like he sat right beside me in the car as I drove. I asked, "You do, Lord?" He answered, "Yes, I do. This is only a state, a temporary place. The people you've lost are okay. They're with me now. Don't worry about them." I began to cry out, "Thank You, Lord! I'm so sorry for questioning you." Once again, I said yes.

I'm sure God has preserved your life countless times as well. This journey is not going to be just highs, there will be valleys as well. There will even be plateaus. In every stage, our job is to say yes to God.

What's Holding You Back?

Some of you need to say "Yes!" You've been running from God, and hiding from the challenge. You've been holding pity parties and holding back your "yes." God is waiting until you agree with him to take you to the wealthy place. He's saying, "I'm going to show you how to get to the wealthy place, as you continually give me all the honor and glory. Just give me your yes."

When I got back to North Carolina, I gathered Ramona and the kids and we prayed. All of us felt released from the emotional burden. God had shown us how to handle challenging times and valleys—by giving him our yes.

Things To Do In A Valley

Ramona and I have discovered that the valley can actually be a productive place, if you know what to do there. Here is what we have learned to do in valleys, by our own experience:

1. Tithe more, give more, and make sure it hurts

Why? Because it affirms again that God is your only supply. Giving prepares your heart for the next time you go to a peak. It builds your confidence on the Rock of Christ. Tithes and giving are a statement of agreement with God. They are a "yes" to His provision and supremacy in all we do. Practice giving in the valley.

2. Spend more

We make our biggest purchases in the valley. We built the home of our dreams in the valley, purchased the building for our business in the valley. You get the best deals in the valley, and we find that we manage everything better there. Only in the valley do we dot every "i" and cross every "t."

Think about it. On the peak you are feeling invincible and emotionally high. When you make big purchases in that frame of mind, you tend to overpay or buy what you don't need. You also make decisions on the faulty assumption that the peak will last forever. Then, when the valley comes, you are in trouble.

Spending in the valley instead of on the peak, teaches you to spend with purpose, not just frivolously and based on our emotions. Make a checklist. Why do you need this purchase? How can you afford it? Will it help you in the low times as well as the high times?

We also spend in the valleys because things are often cheaper there. If everyone is going through an economic valley at the same time, you can find the best deals in the valley. We recently updated our facilities during the so-called recession because labor was cheapest then.

3. Waste less

Most people get careless and wasteful on the peak. When you are in a valley you soon see the waste in your life and business. We have wasted resources in our company—employing people who were not performing up to standard. On the peak you don't see it as well. You think because the company is successful that everyone is working. After all, they look busy! The valley forces you to be more accountable. We have eliminated so much waste in our recent valleys that we are surprised by how much there was. Things we thought were necessary were not. We cut $20,000 a month of expenses we thought we needed, and it did not negatively affect the company or the product. In fact, we are more productive today than ever before.

Where there is ineffective management, God will not provide more resources. When you are on a peak, and perhaps not being careful with your management, God sometimes has to force you to go into a valley so you can say, "I'm listening now."

4. Invest in education

If things ever slow down or seem difficult, invest in yourself during that time. Plant seeds that will bear fruit later when things pick up. Use your time and resources to prepare for the next peak.

Some of you are in a valley right now, and I can hear God saying what he said to me: "Don't stop now. There's a place I am trying to take you. Keep going." To get to the wealthy place you must learn to embrace the valley and always say yes to God.

We have now completed the important principles contained in the word "Wealthy." Next we will move on to the word "Place." In review:

- W = Wake-up!
- E = Educate
- A = Attitude
- L = Leave your old place
- T = Transformed
- H = Hearken
- Y = Say Yes

Passion is about more than possessions or positions. It is about setting goals that make a long-term, meaningful impact on your life and the lives of those around you.

CHAPTER

PURSUE YOUR PASSION!

Now we will study the "P" in the wealthy place: P = Pursue your Passion.

By now you should know that on this journey to the wealthy place you must be ready to fight the fight of faith. The devil will attack you all along the way. You must fight for your marriage, your business, your kids, your peace, and your destiny in Christ. Don't let anybody come and steal God's promises from you.

As soon as you say, "Yes, I'm going to start my own business. Yes, I'm going to make positive changes in my life," it seems like things start breaking down. You ask yourself, "Why does it always happen right after I say 'yes'?" The answer is: because your commitment is being tested. That's the time to get yourself together, dust yourself off and say, "All right. I'm not working with only my own energy anymore. I'm not working with only my own spirit, because my own didn't work in the first place. My own energy, my own belief system, my own "whatever" just didn't work. I need to put all my trust in God because he wants me to pursue his destiny for my life. He's already told me to put on the armor.

Ephesians 6:10–14 NLT

[10] A final word: Be strong in the Lord and in his mighty power.

[11] Put on all of God's armor so that you will be able to stand firm against all strategies of the devil.

[12] For we are not fighting against flesh-and-blood enemies, but against evil rulers and authorities of the unseen world, against mighty powers in this dark world, and against evil spirits in the heavenly places.

[13] Therefore, put on every piece of God's armor so you will be able to resist the enemy in the time of evil. Then after the battle you will still be standing firm.

[14] Stand your ground, putting on the belt of truth and the body armor of God's righteousness.

What God is saying here is, "Now, get yourself ready. We're going to that wealthy place."

What Turns You On?

What is it you love to do? What wakes you up in the morning (beside your kids or your dog)? What gets you excited about each day? Each person has something burning inside—a passion, a drive. Something you love so much, you would do it for no pay whatsoever. Something that you keep putting on the back burner but it keeps jumping to the front burner! That passion is what God is using to show you what to pursue.

Michael: When I was a young man, I worked at the Sheraton hotel. I loved working with people. I was a valet for the car parking service. I parked visitor's cars in the parking structure, and then retrieved those cars when they were ready for them. I tried to be the type of valet who always gave extra service. When people came in, I would go around to the driver's side, open the door and say, "Welcome to the Sheraton. It is my pleasure to welcome you. My name is Michael Woods. If at any time you need assistance, please do not hesitate to call on me." I was the only valet who spoke to visitors like this. I made up my own presentation because I wanted to be original. I said it many times a day, and people seemed to appreciate it. When I brought the cars back, I would open the door for the lady and say, "Ma'am, you have a great evening. Thank you for coming to the Sheraton. If you're ever here again, my name is Michael Woods, and I'd love to serve you." Then I'd open the door for the gentleman, shut the door for him and say, "Sir, thank you for coming to the Sheraton. My name is Michael Woods. If you're ever here again, I'd love to be able to serve you."

That passion caught people's attention. One night, a sharply dressed man and woman came into the hotel. I saw them arrive, but someone else parked their car. When they came out after their event I ran and got the keys, but when I got to their car in the parking structure I was surprised. It was old and raggedy. I thought to myself, *I'm definitely not getting a tip from this guy. No big deal.*

I tried to turn on the car, but it wouldn't start. Having grown up in the country I know how to get tractors and other things started, so I pumped the gas pedal three or four times, turned the ignition and *vroom*, the engine roared to life. I drove that old car around to the entrance, got out, and went back around to open the door for the lady.

She looked beautiful in her nice mink coat, but I couldn't get the passenger door open. I kept pulling on the handle. Finally the gentleman said, "Come over here and try it from the inside." So I went back around to his side, scooted across his seat, and opened her door from the inside. Then I said to the young lady, "Ma'am, my name is Michael Woods. I hope you enjoyed your time here at the Sheraton. If you're ever back in this area again, please do not hesitate to look us up again."

Excellence Always Pays

I knew I wasn't getting a tip—I could tell by the car—but I walked around to the other side and gave the gentleman the same courteous service. I said, "My name is Michael Woods. I hope you had a nice time here. If you're ever back in this area, please look us up again." As he was getting in the car, he handed me something. I shut the door and watched as the car drove off, sputtering, smoke pouring out the back. When he was out of sight I looked in my hand and there was a $50 bill. That was huge to me back then—really huge!

My passion to provide excellent service was rewarded! I learned then that we should never lower our standards or our passion based on circumstance. Stay at a high level of passion. Don't lower it! If you're an eagle, stay an eagle. Don't change into a duck just because of the situation. Continue with the level of excellence God has put in you. Pursue with passion the purpose God has put in your heart.

Meaningful Goals

To pursue means you don't wait for it to come to you. You go after it. King David pursued his purpose. He didn't tell Goliath, "Come to me." He said, "I'm going to Goliath."[1] Sometimes your blessing is waiting for you to go get it. The question is, "Are you going to go?" Don't get stuck at "almost." Don't give up when you're almost there. Stop living almost. God promised it. He already said you can have it. It's up to you to pursue it! Your enthusiasm should light up the people around you.

John 14:13 NLT
You can ask for anything in my name, and I will do it, so that the Son can bring glory to the Father.

---

[1] 1 Samuel 17:41–51

Passion doesn't just burn. It also sets goals. A true goal has several characteristics; does yours?

1. Is it meaningful?

Passion is about more than possessions or positions. It is about setting goals that make a long-term, meaningful impact on your life and the lives of those around you. Passion should be about the biggest things you pursue.

2. Is it yours?

Goals are individually tailored.[2] Never look at someone else's reward. You can mess yourself up when you compare yourself to someone else. If someone else's reward is to go to Hawaii, don't inflict pain on yourself for not being able to afford it yet. You can't let other people's goals haunt you. Don't take their rewards on yourself! It's like getting on someone else's boat. You never know—that boat might be about to sink!

3. Are there long-term benefits?

We talked for years about going to Europe—Paris, Venice, Seville. Years later we visited those cities with our children. As we traveled, we looked back and said, "Wow, we talked about this years ago! Now we're doing it!" Don't look at life as if you have to have it all right now. Some things can wait.

4. Are some of your goals and rewards achievable now?

Before we had any money, we used to dream of going to a place called **Lord Chumley's**, a restaurant we couldn't afford. So we made a plan. Instead of going there for dinner, we went first to **Wendy's** or the **Waffle House**. Then we went to **Lord Chumley's** for dessert. We would order a $15 cheesecake and split it in half.

---

[2] Williams, Dave; *The Miracle of Faith Goals*, Decapolis Publishing, Lansing, MI, 2013, www.faithgoals.com.

It was so good! Other people didn't know we were only having dessert. It felt rewarding to work so hard and have that reward without all the expense. Other times we would stay in a nice hotel for the weekend, checking in early so the kids would have the full experience, and checking out as late as we could. It was a reward we could enjoy on the way to our bigger passion.

5. Is it big enough that it requires God?

This principle is so big that it requires another chapter! It's the story of the biggest step of faith we took in our business career.

In review:

- W = Wake-up!
- E = Educate
- A = Attitude
- L = Leave your old place
- T = Transformed
- H = Hearken
- Y = Say Yes

- P = Pursue your passion

Don't give up when you're almost there.
Stop living "almost."

Home of Ashtae Products, 17 other businesses, Black Network Television, and the BEST business incubator. This building came because we made a decision based on faith, not finances.

CHAPTER

THE BIG STEP

Michael: As the company grew, Ramona and I began looking for a building to purchase. We agreed not to spend a great deal of money on a building, but to get something modest we could fix up over time. Our budget was no more than $300,000 and we wanted around 10,000 square feet. We knew it would have to be an older building—probably a "fixer-upper," since we were working on such a tight budget.

A Diamond in the Rough?

Ramona started looking at different places, and she would call me and say, "I found a building I want you to come look at." I would drive over to take a tour with our real estate agent, and sure enough, she found a lot of fixer-uppers. One place was an old iron and steel shop that was dirty, cold, and in need of a lot of repairs. Ramona called it a diamond in the rough; I just called it rough, but I didn't share my true feelings with her so as not to dampen her excitement. It was true that the price was well within our budget.

But one day on the way to work, I passed a building that had a sign out front: **Salvation Army Toy Pickup Location.** I went in to see it; a man sitting there explained to me that this building was being used temporarily for an annual toy giveaway. As I walked around this empty warehouse, I heard God speaking to me in one ear and my wife speaking to me in the other. God would say, "Isn't this a wonderful place? Think of all you could do with this space." Ramona, figuratively speaking into my other ear, followed with, "This is way beyond us. What are you even doing in this building? Get out of there before you get too attached to it. Remember what we discussed? The budget, the square footage and what we could afford?" God would respond, "You know I can do all things, right?"[1]

> **Luke 1:37 AMP**
> For with God nothing is ever impossible and no word from God shall be without power or impossible of fulfillment.
>
> **Mark 9:23 NLT**
> "What do you mean, 'If I can'?" Jesus asked. "Anything is possible if a person believes."

This inner battle raged on as I kept walking through the massive warehouse. Each time I pulled back a huge steel sliding door, I could imagine how that space would function if we bought it. This room would be the educational center. This area could be for new small businesses to get started. After a while, I could not hear my wife's voice anymore, only what God was telling me about the new building. I walked around that building for at least an hour, dreaming and talking with God.

If you are married, you already know that just because you had a talk with God, your spouse may not have been in on that same conversation. In fact, your spouse may interpret reality very differently. I couldn't wait to share the good news with Ramona, but I knew I had to do my homework first and learn all the

---

[1] Mark 9:23 NLT; Luke 18:27 NLT

details. I also should locate the nearest insane asylum, because she may want to check me in as a patient.

Have You Lost Your Mind?

Sure enough, when I took her on a tour I heard the five magic words: "Have you lost your mind?"

Ramona had no initial excitement, no enthusiasm, and no interest after seeing how large this place was. She was calculating how we could afford this place—and the answer was: we couldn't. If you haven't noticed by now, Ramona and I have different roles in our company. She is the CFO and sees the actual money that comes in and what goes out. She can tell you which account has enough money in it for project A, B, or C. She is very good at her role. Without her skills and guidance, we would not be in business.

I, on the other hand, work slightly differently. I visualize where we can be and want to fill in the details later.

Ramona: I walked around that building in shock that Michael would even propose such a place. It was much larger than we needed—47,000 square feet, when we were only looking for 10,000. Our facility at the time was just 5,000 square feet, so this was almost ten times larger. I knew we couldn't afford it and there was no reason to jump to such a large building. Still, Michael kept saying, "We'll have this here, that there. Double crown molding, nine-inch base boards, businesses here and there." All I was hearing was, "The building costs this, to update it will cost this, the mortgage is this, amortization is this, interest is that." My conclusion: There was no way we could afford the building, let alone the renovations. We would have to spend at least half a million on top of the $2 million purchase price.

Michael, of course, didn't hear any of my objections because he believed God was in it. He always talked about how building on faith is more powerful than relying on the bankers or the economy. He was totally convinced that God had shown him this place and that it would be our new business home.

Ephesians 3:20 NLT
Now all glory to God, who is able, through his mighty power at work within us, to accomplish infinitely more than we might ask or think.

I was thinking, *Lord, when are you going to speak to me? Why do you only talk to Michael about these big visions? Don't you remember what we just came out of? My husband doesn't care how much this costs or where the money's coming from to pay for it. You've got to talk some sense into him!*

When God Gives the Vision

But when God gives someone a vision, they can't let it go. I know when Michael has a hunch, a wish, or a vision that God has put in him. I don't ever like it. It's uncomfortable. But it's what takes us to the next level. You need to deal with what God can do. In many businesses or partnerships you have the far-sighted person and the near-sighted person. Michael is the far-sighted person, the visionary. He doesn't see what's in front of him. He only sees what is in the distance, and he wants to get there. I am the near-sighted person who sees all the details. You need both. If you only have far-sighted people you can get yourself in trouble. But as the near-sighted person, you have to be willing to embrace a bigger vision than you can believe for.[2]

We never crunched numbers about the building, never went over the finances together. I just trusted that Michael was hearing from God. We slid a $141,000 check across the desk at the bank and got that building. All I can say is, "Thank God," because it

---

[2] 2 Corinthians 4:18 KJV

was not us who made it work. In the natural we didn't have the money. But if we had operated according to what was in our bank account, we would be in a smaller place today and probably have a smaller, less effective company. Instead, that massive building now hosts seventeen businesses, an event center, Black Network Television studios, a courtyard, and our own company, Ashtae. It's all part of making decisions based on faith, not finances.

When you pursue your passion, don't rely on marketplace studies. Rely on your vision. Your business is as big as you want it to be. Yes, pursuing your passion can be scary! Sometimes it forcibly disconnects you from the comfort you cling to. But we have learned more and more to pursue our passions together. They drive us, wake us up in the morning, and make us excited to live each day.

How about you? Are you pursuing something with that kind of passion?

Nobody gets to the wealthy place without
first passing through the fire.

10

LOVE WHAT YOU LIVED THROUGH

Ramona: The next letter in wealthy place is "L." L = Love.

Whatever you've been through, whatever you've done, the mistakes you've made, the bad decisions you have lived through, it's time to do something radical: you have to love what you've been through. Love the stuff you have gone through—every bit of it. Once you embrace every mistake and failure, God can turn it around for your benefit.

Why? Because when you embrace it and accept everything that has happened to you, God has a way of making it *all* good.[1] This is why the Bible says,

James 1:2 NLT
Dear brothers and sisters, when troubles come your way, consider it an opportunity for great joy.

Count it all joy. It does not say, "Count only the good times as joy." No—count it *all* as joy!

---
[1] Romans 8:28 KJV

Burning Hotter Than You Can Stand?

As you know by now, we have been through painful, dark days. But so have you. You must come to the place where you love that you went through a difficult process. All God was doing was putting you in the fire and taking you out. Putting you in and taking you out. He does it to refine and strengthen your reliance on him. Every time he puts you in the fire, it feels like you are burning hotter than you can stand. But unless you go through and learn to love those times, you won't arrive at the wealthy place.

People living in the wealthy place appear happy and content, but you don't see their yesterdays. They have joy because they count it all joy, the good and the bad and the ugly. Nobody gets to the wealthy place without first passing through the fire.

Michael: I remember going through a fire of my own making in Buffalo. Every day I would go to work, park illegally in front of our building, and get a parking ticket. In Buffalo, it seems like you can't park anywhere, and we had all these beauty salons we were trying to make deliveries to. I got so many parking tickets that I hid them from my wife. Finally the city threatened to put a boot on my car and impound it. My mind-set was that I would get around to paying the tickets sometime. There were so many— what did one more matter?

Around that time, I bought four brand new Michelin tires for my Delta '88 automobile. I came to work to grab a few boxes of product to take with me on the road. Then the phone rang and I talked to Ramona longer than I expected. When I came back outside I saw a strange yellow device on my tire—a boot. *How dare they put a boot on my car*, I thought, *here I am trying to go to work and make a living for my family. How dare they do that?* I was mad at the entire state of New York. A sticker on the window told me, "This Car Will be Towed." I thought, *Oh no they're not!* I got my keys out, opened the trunk, took out my jack, jacked up the car, went behind the building to get some cinder blocks, put them under the car and took all the other tires off the car. I said, "If they're taking this car, at least they won't get my new tires." I took all three tires inside.

Sure enough, the city came and towed it. I had to pay $1,000 to get it back, plus all the parking ticket fees. I was so upset that I let the car sit in impound for about a month, as if that was hurting anyone but me.

"Stuck on Stupid!"

I was "stuck on stupid," as we say. I was flat wrong. I was in the fire, but not learning the lesson that would get me out of it. Sometimes it takes a while to come to your senses. Finally I came to mine, paid all my tickets, and stopped parking illegally. Did I love paying all that money and being angry with the city? No. Do I love the lessons I learned from that and the changes it caused in my own character? Absolutely!

That was a fire of my own design, but sometimes God puts you in a fire that you can't get out of until he says you're done.[2] That fire refines you. Sustained pressure turns you into a diamond. Don't be wimpy! See it all the way through and you will come out stronger, more effective, and wealthier than before.

---

[2] Malachi 3:2–7 KJV

When you fly, the ride isn't always smooth…rising to higher
levels may bring turbulence. But striving to go higher, in spite of
the bumps, leads to bigger rewards.

11

ALTITUDE

Michael: Not only must you learn to love what you lived through, you must maintain your altitude through vigilance in avoiding complacency. The next letter in place is "A" = Altitude. Every time Ramona and I get complacent, the challenge to regain our altitude usually comes in the area of finances. Money is one of the great indicators of how high we are flying in faith. When we feel stingy, we know we are losing altitude. When we freely give as we have freely received, we know we're doing okay.

Ramona: I was raised by a Catholic mother and an atheist father. My father did not allow any of us to go to church. He only allowed my mom to have candles and saints in a closet, and she would go and worship privately. As a child I would see her do that and hear her saying, "En nombre de Jesus…" But she was not allowed to teach us to worship. I graduated from high school and had never been to church. I moved to North Carolina and a friend invited me to a place called Friendship Church. That's when I first visited a church.

Michael has strong roots in Christianity. Tithing was normal for him, even when our home was being foreclosed. Michael always says, "God will provide. He'll beat us to the bank." The humorous thing is that God never let our tithe checks bounce, though other checks were bouncing like crazy. I call that a divine sense of humor.

Malachi 3:8–12 NLT

[8] "Should people cheat God? Yet you have cheated me! "But you ask, 'What do you mean? When did we ever cheat you?' "You have cheated me of the tithes and offerings due to me.

[9] You are under a curse, for your whole nation has been cheating me.

[10] Bring all the tithes into the storehouse so there will be enough food in my Temple. If you do," says the Lord of Heaven's Armies, "I will open the windows of heaven for you. I will pour out a blessing so great you won't have enough room to take it in! Try it! Put me to the test!

[11] Your crops will be abundant, for I will guard them from insects and disease. Your grapes will not fall from the vine before they are ripe," says the Lord of Heaven's Armies.

[12] "Then all nations will call you blessed, for your land will be such a delight," says the Lord of Heaven's Armies.

Philippians 4:19 NLT

And this same God who takes care of me will supply all your needs from his glorious riches, which have been given to us in Christ Jesus.

One particular Sunday, Michael was out of town and I was at church with the girls. Michael always let me know how much I was supposed to write the tithe check for. This particular week he forgot to leave instructions for me. A guest minister was speaking that Sunday and he said, "There are 10 people here who are supposed to write a check for $1,000." I had never written a check for $1,000 to a church. I *knew* I wasn't one of the people he was talking to. But as I sat there a voice inside of me said, "You need to write that check." I answered, "Are you talking to me?" Again that voice said, "You're supposed to write that check."

A Battle Over Giving

I began battling within myself. How could I do something I had never done before—especially without Michael's agreement? It was a scary amount for me to just give away based on what I thought I heard. But I recognized that voice. The Holy Spirit was speaking to my heart. Finally, I got out the pen and started writing. My hand was trembling so much my writing was shaky. I was so scared. I got up and handed that check in. I didn't hear anything the rest of the service, because my internal dialogue kept me from hearing the message: *Oh, Ramona. What have you done?*

As soon as I got out of church I called Michael. "You'll never believe what I just did. This minister was there, and he said there were ten people who were supposed to write a check for $1,000 dollars. Something inside of me told me to write a check. And I wrote it." Michael simply said, "All right. No problem."

That day freed me. I did not know that all the years before I was paying tithes strictly out of obedience to my husband. It wasn't because I believed in tithing or because I had the same conviction he had. That day was the turning point. I had my first true encounter with the Holy Spirit about money. Interestingly, we were praying to build a million-dollar business, but I was afraid to write a $1,000 check. It's amazing how you can believe God for great things to bless you, but get stuck in "low-giving" mode when it comes to your own generosity.

Today, we talk about tithing and giving generously when we speak in church settings and corporate settings. It's a key. Tithing teaches you self-discipline and it yanks you out of the complacent place. When you find yourself flying at a lower altitude in your faith or finances, do something that only God can cover. Give a gift that "hurts." It only hurts until you receive the promised harvest when it comes. That's how you gain altitude.

Michael: I fly all the time, and I have noticed that whenever you increase altitude it seems to create some turbulence. Turbulence usually comes with breaking through to another level. When you fly a while at that altitude, it's smooth flying. Then you fly higher again and battle a little more turbulence along the way.

That's a picture of what it's like to get to the wealthy place. As you rise to higher levels of success by overcoming the problems, situations, and obstacles you face, you will experience turbulence. That's okay. A few bumps are worth it when you finally arrive!

What It All Means

To live in the wealthy place means that money is no longer an issue. You are only a conduit that God's resources flow through. Money flows through you to advance God's kingdom on earth.

For example, we have helped hundreds of kids in our community through our foundation that supports them academically. The **Jessa-Maria Foundation** is a charitable organization dedicated to empowering and educating minority youth on the importance of higher education, financial literacy, business, and entrepreneurship. Many of the kids don't pass their aptitude tests, so we invest time and energy into them. It is really God investing in them through us. We tell them, "Look, you can be successful." We bring them to our campus and show them the salons, accounting firms, karate studio, television studio, and the many other types of businesses there. We try to teach them what is possible if you do things God's way.

Because we don't "hang on" to God's resources, he continues to bless us with more than enough. He knows we will be faithful to sow seeds into his kingdom—and that blesses him and thereby God also blesses us!

We also partner with **Strategic Global Mission**[1] (SGM), Dr. Dave Williams' charitable giving ministry. SGM is a non-profit corporation with the sole purpose of accelerating the Gospel of Jesus Christ through targeted grants, scholarships, missions, and pastoral education. Grants are provided to selected non-profit ministries who focus on "at risk" children and inner-city ministries whose goal is to reach and minister to children.

We have faith that God is faithful. When we are generous to his causes, we are always blessed in return. You can maintain your "altitude" through your generosity.

In review:

- W = Wake-up!
- E = Educate
- A = Attitude
- L = Leave your old place
- T = Transformed
- H = Hearken
- Y = Say Yes

- P = Pursue your passion
- L = Love what you lived through
- A = Altitude

---

[1] www.strategicglobalmission.com

Once you commit to God wholeheartedly, he will show up and show off in any situation you encounter.

12

COMMIT TO THE BATTLE!

The "C" in wealthy place stands for "Commit to the battle." We like to say a little prayer to remind us of God's faithfulness and our commitment to him. It comes from the lyrics of a gospel song entitled: *You've Been So Faithful,* by Eddie James.[1]

Dear Heavenly Father,

As I look back over my life, I can see how your love has guided me. Even though I've done wrong, you've never left me alone. But you forgave me, and you kept on blessing me. This I recall to my mind. Therefore I have hope. It is because of your mercy that I am not consumed.

Thy compassions do not fail. They are new every morning. Great is thy faithfulness! You've been so faithful, even though I haven't done everything I am supposed to do. Even though I haven't said everything I am sup-

---

[1] James, Eddie & Knight, Bradley; *You've Been So Faithful*, Brentwood-Benson Publishing, Emeryville, CA, 94608.

*posed to say. Your faithfulness has guided me and brought me
to a wonderful place. I thank you, God.*

~Amen!

Once you commit to God wholeheartedly, he will show up and
show off in any situation you encounter. Ephesians talks about a
shield of faith as part of the armor of God.

Ephesians 6:10–18 CEV

[10] Finally, let the mighty strength of the Lord make
you strong.

[11] Put on all the armor that God gives, so you can defend
yourself against the devil's tricks.

[12] We are not fighting against humans. We are fighting
against forces and authorities and against rulers of darkness
and powers in the spiritual world.

[13] So put on all the armor that God gives. Then when that evil
day comes, you will be able to defend yourself. And when
the battle is over, you will still be standing firm.

[14] Be ready! Let the truth be like a belt around your waist,
and let God's justice protect you like armor.

[15] Your desire to tell the good news about peace should be
like shoes on your feet.

[16] Let your faith be like a shield, and you will be able to stop
all the flaming arrows of the evil one.

[17] Let God's saving power be like a helmet, and for a sword
use God's message that comes from the Spirit.

[18] Never stop praying, especially for others. Always pray by
the power of the Spirit. Stay alert and keep praying for
God's people.

When you are heading toward the wealthy place, it's not
always easy. Anyone who thinks that way is terribly mistaken.
You must wear the right armor. The helmet of salvation, the
breastplate of righteousness, the belt of truth, the sword of the
Holy Spirit, your feet must be shod with the preparation of the
Gospel of peace—and the shield of faith. Sometimes your faith

reservoir gets low, leaving you unprepared for battle. How big is your shield today? If little things stop you, annoy you, bring out your complaining side, then your faith is dwindling and you are vulnerable in battle.

Prepare for Battle

Don't let anybody kid you. It is a battle to get to the wealthy place. You must be prepared to fight. If you want what God wants for you, you've got to go for it with everything you have. Not only will you find blessings for you and your family, but you will bring blessings to others. We like to say that our business brings us in the back door. Our clients think we're there to sell hair care products, but our most important goal is to tell them about Jesus Christ and God's Kingdom. We have a product we want to talk about first, because it opens the door for us. Once we get in, we build relationships and are able to tell them about the Gospel.

Only strong, vibrant faith gives you the confidence to win souls. If you've got your wimpy gear on, you are definitely not ready for battle. If you aren't ready to fight, it is easier to be on welfare and wait for the check. You don't need any faith to be poor. Zero! But poverty-land is not the place you want to be.

Get committed! Get out your shield of faith and God will use you to do amazing things.

Michael and Ramona believe God has called you to live in the wealthy place. They pray for your success and would love to hear from you.

13

CHAPTER

EMBRACE

We have reached the final letter in wealthy place: E = Embrace. Embrace your God-given vision; embrace your talents; embrace the idea that God wants you to be wealthy!

It's time to embrace those talents inside of you. It's okay to be wealthy. Stop convincing yourself there's something wrong with it. It's a good thing, a great thing, to go to the wealthy place. God will bless you, and many others through you, as you are faithful to the journey.

What Am I Going to Do?

One day, a customer came to our office. She was crying. You could see the emotion on her face, and she insisted on speaking with us. So, we came out to speak with her. We sat down with her and she said, "My business is going down, I'm losing customers. My husband was diagnosed with cancer. We don't have any insurance. What am I going to do?"

We sat there thinking, *should we write her a check? Or can we do something to help her change her situation on her own?* Something came over Michael and he said, "Friend, pull yourself together.

Make some flyers—as many as you can—and hand out a hundred every day. Get to your salon early and clean up the place. Make it somewhere people want to go. The only way out of the situation you are in now is to look to God to help you to do something right."

He even made her practice handing out flyers right there in the conference room! He was helping her to embrace the vision she had lost along the way. A handout wasn't going to help her get to the wealthy place. So many people focus on what got them into the problem, telling everyone about it, singing that same old song. How you got there doesn't matter. We all have a story we could tell to a violin accompaniment. Instead, embrace the original vision you enjoyed before you got into the ditch. Connecting with that vision again will get you out quicker than focusing on the mess.

Two months later, that woman came and thanked us for helping her out of the mess and mind-set she was in. Everywhere she went she handed out flyers. She had hope again, and her life and success were rebounding. That heavy spirit of defeat was gone, and she was on her way to better things. When you step out in faith with God holding your hand, you will experience success!

As we said before, statistically we are not supposed to be where we are right now. But when you have God in your life, the world's "statistics" don't apply. His purpose is greater than any numbers. He has taken us—two simple people—and is using us to do his will. We don't always reach the mark, but we embrace this journey to the wealthy place every day. Why? Because we want people to say, "Michael and Ramona gave it their all. They went great places with God and helped others to go along, too."

We believe the principles in this book are more than enough to help you get started on your journey to the wealthy place.

Remember:

- W = Wake-up!
- E = Educate
- A = Attitude
- L = Leave your old place
- T = Transformed
- H = Hearken
- Y = Say yes

- P = Pursue your passion
- L = Love what you lived through
- A = Altitude
- C = Commit to the battle
- E = Embrace

Never forget, God has given YOU the power to get wealth,[1] when you covenant with him through his Son, Jesus![2]

We'd love to hear from you. We'd love to hear your story of how this book has impacted your life; our contact information is in the next page of this book. May God richly bless you as you step-by-step travel into the wealthy place!

---

[1] Deuteronomy 8:18
[2] Ephesians 3:20

CONTACT INFORMATION

Michael and Ramona Woods
Black Network Television
1325 South Eugene St
Greensboro, NC 27406

Phone:
336-404-1033

Email & Web:
mwoods@blacknetworktelevision.com
www.blacknetworktelevision.com

Decapolis Publishing
P.O. Box 80825
Lansing, MI 48908-0825

Phone:
800-888-7284
517-731-0000

Web:
www.decapolisbooks.com
www.club52.com

About Michael & Ramona Woods

Michael and Ramona Woods have been married for over 22 years and are the parents of two daughters, Taylore and Ashley. They cofounded Ashtae Products, Inc., (named after their two daughters) in 1994. Ashtae Products is one of the leading distributors of multicultural hair care products to beauty salons all over the USA, Canada, and the Caribbean Islands.

Michael, a veteran of the US Army Reserves, attended four years at North Carolina Agricultural & Technical State University in Greensboro, NC, while Ramona received her Associates Degree from Brevard College in Brevard, NC.

The Woods are coauthors of the book *Against the Grain*. They are highly sought after motivational and inspirational speakers at conferences and churches around the world.

Michael and Ramona's most recent project was the launch of the first African-American television station in the state of North Carolina. In 2011, **Black Network Television (BNT)** was born. Through excellence in the broadcast industry, BNT has a mission to provide a voice for a community that has not been heard, show a picture of a community that has not been shown, and tell the story of a community that has yet to be told.

As serial entrepreneurs, the Woods purchased a 47,000 square foot, dilapidated warehouse in an economically challenged neighborhood and remodeled it into a five-acre pristine campus that houses twenty-one independent entrepreneurs, Galleria Events Center, Ashtae Products, Black Network Television, and the North Carolina Agricultural & Technical State University Business Entrepreneurial Skills Training business incubator. The two are passionate about helping people to balance faith, family, and finances in order to reach their full God-given potential.

MORE **LIFE CHANGING**
PRODUCTS FROM **DECAPOLIS PUBLISHING**

8⁹⁵

Miracle Breakthrough Power of the First Fruit

This offering has the power to launch success, attract blessings, and make God an enemy to your enemies. Let Dr. Dave Williams show you how to unleash God's astonishing blessings!

80 PAGES

9⁹⁵

The Miracle of Faith Goals

God plans for everything—from when he spoke forth the universe, to his plan for your salvation, all the way to this moment in your life. This book reveals God's plan for accomplishing great things. You will learn the seven "Vs", incremental steps, that will help you accomplish 100 to 1,000 times more!

135 PAGES

13⁹⁵

Coming into The Wealthy Place

God wants you to be wealthy—few discover the wealthy place. As a believer, you might think that God encourages a spirit of "poverty." Nothing could be further from the truth! God wants you to prosper by connecting to the Great Commission, so you can accomplish his will on earth.

170 PAGES

Select titles available on:

Shop **decapolisbooks.com** or call 1-800-888-7284